To Alis

with every good wish,

David

D.A. Johnson was born in Cheshire, and lived his early life in Oldham, Lancashire, where he attended the Hulme Grammar School. He has been an event organiser, and sold Balinese carvings from a market stall. He is now a Senior Psychiatric Social Worker and Therapist in mental health services in the West Midlands.

UNDER THE LONE NIGHT

D. A. Johnson

UNDER THE LONE NIGHT

Vanguard Press

VANGUARD PAPERBACK

© Copyright 2012
D. A. Johnson

The right of D. A Johnson to be identified as author of
this work has been asserted by him in accordance with the
Copyright, Designs and Patents Act 1988.

All Rights Reserved

No reproduction, copy or transmission of this publication
may be made without written permission.
No paragraph of this publication may be reproduced,
copied or transmitted save with the written permission of the publisher, or
in accordance with the provisions
of the Copyright Act 1956 (as amended).

Any person who commits any unauthorised act in relation to
this publication may be liable to criminal
prosecution and civil claims for damages.

A CIP catalogue record for this title is
available from the British Library.

ISBN 978 1 843868 33 0

*Vanguard Press is an imprint of
Pegasus Elliot MacKenzie Publishers Ltd.*
www.pegasuspublishers.com

First Published in 2012

**Vanguard Press
Sheraton House Castle Park
Cambridge England**

Printed & Bound in Great Britain

Disclaimer

The personages in these poems are creations of imagination, as are their names. Any resemblance to actual persons, living or dead is purely coincidental.

For Sandrea

Contents

Ad Astra	15
Alien Moon	17
Arrows	18
Assessment	19
Beech Alley	21
Black Rock Sands	22
Bodybuilder	23
Butterflies	24
Costa Blanca	26
De Profundis	28
DNA	30
Dover 1962	32
Dudley Castle March 19th	33
Fils a Papa	35
Funeralia	37
Iceland	39
Imago Joannis	40
Jack	41
Knowledge	43
Le Pari	44
Lyonesse	46
Maker	47
Margarite	49
Margery Daw	50
Monster	52
Mousehole	53
Musee des Beaux Arts	54

Mystery	55
New World	56
Overlooking the Lake	58
Palace of the Winds	59
Passive Voice	61
Patient O	62
Paul	63
Pilgrimage	65
Praeterita	66
Prisoners Request	67
Revelation	68
Saturn Return	69
Secrets	70
Sic Placet	72
Side Ward	74
Species of Oblivion	76
Spring	77
The Ancients knew	78
The Lane at Glenmore	79
The Power of Meaning	80
Tree	82
Tremadog Bay August 30th	83
Untitled	85
Untitled (2)	86
Untitled (3)	88
Valencia	89
Visiting Time	91
"Vous etes Belge, Monsieur?"	92
Wheel	93
Zu ende	94
Mot Juste	95
Elgar Girl	96

Ad Astra

The Jasmines
of Rosemont Park
NJ,
innocent of Ozymandias,
and even
Ecclesiastes,
decide to make their mark.
Jim
driven on like Tamburlaine's
jades
climbs the ladder at Citibank.
(Futures).
Georgy
who brought forth men children only,
teaches the gifted,
her own Wechsler score
nowhere to be found.
Their place in the Berkshires
is not like Herzog's.
More exclusive,
in a forested
development.
They get away
whenever they can.
But thinking of

her psychology professor
in Paris last year,
Georgy's eyes are dead
in the mirror
as she ascends
the Mass Pike.
Playing Scrabble
at Tanglewood
Jim still spells sou
with two "o"s.
At the Democratic Convention
they sat fifteen places
from Jimmy Carter.
If only they could get
a place on the Park.

Alien Moon

Where do you stand
when all has been taken?
Where do you pray
when cathedrals fall?
Courage must sneer
and spit on forsaken,
but the truth is
that bread has rotted to gall.
Weaving the weave
of gaining's endeavour,
the harridan bride
and child as a thief,
put a stone to the cairn
of tiny forever
and a knife to the heart
of days held in fief.
Tomorrow turns habit
and stands to the lee
of an alien moon rising
on an alien sea.

Arrows

Sometimes I feel
we are arrows in flight.
We did not meet the archer,
we know not where we land.
We did not fix on peace or war,
or guide the fletcher's hand.
Some tarry in the quiver
or perish in the store,
some are snapped in two for policy,
all are predelict to gore.
Many feel their course is brief,
bred by habit, loosed for sport.
Once fired no luxury
of philosophy,
no opportunity of retort.
Some say we met the archer
and know where we will land,
some say we cast
for peace or war
to guide the fletcher's hand.

Assessment

The three wise monkeys
stood upon her rug.
The kindness of their hearts
hid the treachery
of their smiles.
Had she been
hearing voices?
Did she think people
were against her?
She might as well have sat
before a tank.
She had no rifle
nor a flower,
no placard nor brave mob
in support.
The armies of reply
were absent.
If only the air cav
had come in firing
to ask their
settled opinion
between cupping
and the casting out
of demons,
insulin comas

and the major neuroleptics.
She would have smiled
kindly,
asked them to take
their time
and tell about
tardive dyskinesia
and the exact mechanism
of ECT.

Beech Alley

Down the alley of autumnal beeches
surely a figure
towards the far end?
A woman's form
but indistinct,
certainly no face to be made out.
Is the figure retreating
or still in thought, sorrow
contemplation?
A quiet object
of desire and repose
no more to be visited
than a star.
Sought after seeking
till the Dionysian night
when running down the street
catching and leaving,
"Are you, are you?"
Surely that is what the artist
meant to say?

Black Rock Sands

Glistening strand mirroring
the sky and clouds,
seeming at the sea's edge
as wide as the wild air.
Ruined Criccieth behind,
Snowdon before,
a gleaming present framing
past and future in
the stretched dimensions
of creation.
How many rags
and tags
have been discarded here,
how many resolves
hammered into something new?
Gods and daimons
greeted,
loves
put aside.
Before freedom
the winds tell
you are here.

Bodybuilder

Gasp strain shift heft,
lie roll flex heave,
crouch and agonising
stand.
Pain fort et dure
David de Michel-Ange
might form.
Thighs that will not
cross and arms that
hold back the ghetto's
unblinking eye.
Dorsals and abdomen
enthral
the methadone Venus
but in the perfumed watches
of a hot night,
she hears him whimper
as the bar room fight
is lost.

Butterflies

Butterfly
how seminal
a tale,
the Hellespont
ever scanned
for a Leander
who never
returns.
Maxine
a handmaiden
of Radiology
wounded
but did not bring home
her Professor.
After forty years
of watching men
from her parents'
window,
vowed to write
no more letters,
vowed,
but could not stop.
"I thought after Dad died
he would come up more.
London is not so far

these days."
And so she waits
to join
the unravish'd brides
of quietness.

Costa Blanca

Out of Torrevieja
on the coast
to the south,
below
the Zenia Hotel,
the last of the Norman Price's
blood
is spent
beaten from his head
on Acton High Street
on two
whiskey sours,
by Frankie Francis.
Taking the concrete
walkway along
the beach beneath
a hundred million years
of sea life
now dry
as an ex-pat's
heart,
his girlfriend
unable to face
the sunrise
yet again

feels
in the pit of her
stomach
that Cartagena
ought
to be destroyed.

De Profundis

The reading
at evensong
in the February dark.
Is a moiety
wide of the mark?
The Face of God.
Verses trite
as a Stratford-upon-Avon
brass knight.
Sinking suns
and infants hands,
spangled skies
and wedding bands.
Rather
the priest's
Christmas dream
of the sweeper
who came in alarm.
"What am I to do?
Beneath the grit
and blowing papers
of the street,
I have found
a human face."
Below the walls

the dreary and bitter
men shy
to embrace.
Absent from
transcended calms,
a world sustained
on aching arms.

DNA

In Bank Holiday week,
the crowds
now thinning,
the proletariat
grateful for the National Trust
arrive by Ford Prefect
in the car park
to regard
in vitro
lives eugenically perfected.
Admirals
and diplomats
smiling over the Beckstein
in Belgrade,
the sons
in a smart cavalry regiment,
blemishes dimmed
by miles of gravel
and sugar money.
Dotty old Nurse,
on the second floor
(privately cared for)
gets loose occasionally
when the agency nurse
nods off,

likes to point out
where the babies are buried.
No incineration
or stem cell research
here.
You can see it
from the tea shop.

Dover 1962

Fourteen years old
in Kent still a garden.
New mown grass from
Dover College field beneath
Spitfires, not long gone.
From the hill behind Shakespeare Cliff
I watch the ferries come and go.
At night, cars descend
the Canterbury Road –
did they swerve for the ghostly nun?
And wait, and wait.
Along the sea front
wait
beneath the lighted Gateway Flats
for places rumoured, glimpsed.
At dawn
Ernie and Beattie Burrage,
sixty, nut-brown and leather-hard
bicycle off to pick hops.
Gulls scream over cliff
and castle.
A world in a Gauloise.
Can promise ever exceed this?

Dudley Castle March 19th

Cerulean
eyefall
to walls and towers
long sundered
twix from twain.
Fortress no longer fort,
keep no longer kept,
true Star Chamber
and Jerusalem
here:
where
the bright integument
of air
turned furious
out does the wolves
below,
and brings its oceanic weight
to bear.
Howls above
howls beneath
hurls aloft
into the teeth
of the wind
last autumn's
leavings

blinding
the bright sun's
watering eye
and not
by and by
but in a twinkle
like fish diving
they plunge below
where the secret waters
go
and in that
subterranean lee
find the foundings
of an ancient sea.

Fils a Papa

Seb sleeps poorly,
despite the Zopiclone
and vodka.
In tachycardic dreams
he sees the bypass
where the works once stood.
Billy Chen says
"Waster,"
and puts down the phone.
Son of a Grand Master,
some members of the craft
no longer take his calls.
Jap fibre optics
was the coup de grace,
the Japs, and sacrifices
to the great god Dionysus.
And the boy
born to four point five
now weeps
for the loss of thirty grand.
The bill
for yesterday's shoot
lies unpaid on the table.
Four grand
plus v.a.t.

And only one of dad's
Purdeys
is required
for the final
asymmetry.

Funeralia

A mass was said for Rosa.
Many people came.
The husband
who slashed your tyres
when you parted
comforted your youngest
in the front row.
The lover
who would not leave his wife
sat ten rows behind.
The priest
with whom you would not
leave your child alone
told us
we are born in sin.
But all wore black
sang the hymns,
sat in the candles'
quiet light.
All faced the casket,
could not credit
your sudden absence,
sat beneath

the immensity of death.
And from what distant shore
did you watch
those for a moment
made one for you?

Iceland

gem on
the seam of the world.
waste perch thunder
flood and flow
where risen fire cooled
and kissed
fold fall
torque and torsion.
No geomancer envy
stay the far awe
of peak and living ice,
vast ash and cinder lay
and strike carillion
to the river piled
where God the articifer
may be alone
hearing only
the prayers
of the Earth.

And slowly drips
obsidian.

Imago Joannis

Down past Tillich
and Kierkegaard,
past Kant
and Descartes,
tumbling tumbling
helter skelter,
grasping but not catching
at Aquinas,
hurtling past Plato
and You Know Who,
past the pre-Socratics
and the nameless sages,
past the origin of language,
(big one that)
you arrive
at the Hulton Picture Library
of the numinous,
and the possibility of reply
to many a query
formed or not,
a screwdriver
in positivism's eye.

Jack

Like most spirits,
your visit is oblique,
usually a memory,
entirely out of place.
And why
do you come tonight?
After the limestone trickle
of understanding,
to show the same sea floor
from which we grew?
Your time was before
mitigations,
none asked, none given.
That sat ill
with softer souls,
women, children.
All the gaucheries
of a good heart
set to your debit.
Pride, silence
and fumbling with a new world
turned the final keys.
And now

like an exchange of prisoners
forgiveness is rendered
over a barrier neither may cross.

Knowledge

Endings do not seem
to be the issue.
Whether space curves round
or just goes on,
just what God
had in mind
when he planted
the garden.
A place
on which to stand
always seems
to be a problem.
Fields medallists
are brawling in
the alley.
Philosophers
get to sixty
and need
valium.
But
I can hear Hilversum
more clearly
and get to New York
in five minutes.

Le Pari

Standing in the Casino des Nobles,
thinking on the odds,
(red or black, red or black).
How many galaxies did you say,
Mr Hubble?
Should that be
factored in at all?
The dance floor where
Gaia and Goldilocks
entrance.
The child's smile,
the picture of all those
we have ever loved.
Should sentimentality
be strained from the equation,
whose other terms
are shipwrecks and schizophrenia?
The House habitués claim
to know a thing or two.
The staff
are the worst.

You don't have to be
a prophet
to dream where the ball
will land.

Lyonesse

The golden west,
beginning at the Tor.
Ask some physicist
what are the properties
of Lyonesse?
Did Watkins
and star children
in painted vans
dream Gaia's
neurology?
Or do airs blow softer,
trees bend stranger,
porpoises keep nearer,
trancers sink deeper?
I only remember
a place of awakenings,
beneath wakeful gulls
and the cousin stars.

Maker

Grumbling and muttering,
spilling crumbs of bread
and drops of wine,
You make your way
through darkness
by candlelight.
Outside stillness, darkness,
the calm of night.
You climb
the creaking ladder
to the gallery,
lie slowly back
with aching limbs.
Lighting more candles
you regard
with joy and despair.
Some paint spilled,
You carefully mix
and look again.
Taking up a brush
You stare
without moving.
Your hand
pauses
for an age.

Then beginning
again,
You no more know
the end
than Your creation.

Margarite

Once again in your lotus sleep,
with your head on the arm of the chair.
A Venus of the flies,
a variety of fair.
Will you wake this evening?
Who of us can tell?
Your child plays in Tunisia,
or might as well.
Does space have a fabric
or is a void a void?
Can you pluck salvation
from what has been enjoyed?
Look on the arctic of your days
find a speck of precious true,
and make to pause the lookers on
who once had pictures of you.

Margery Daw

See saw Margery Daw
has proved
unsatisfactory.
Return her
to the factory.
Get another one.
Just like the other one?
Complain
about the line.
Supervisor says
the line is fine.
Tell him
the bi-polarity
of the gender
can be a serious
ender.
Supervisor says
"Adjust your focus.
All this hocus pocus
about sparrows,
individuality ends
at the barrows.
My concern
is for the kind.
For after geology

comes biology.
Survival and reproduction
are supplied.
All other privileges
are denied."

Monster

The playground taunts
and kicks,
the laughter
and the chanting,
slowly drained the mercy
from him
like blood
from a butchered sow.
The street contumely
of strangers
brought his soul
to a left hand
turn.
So when
the ugly weight
was gone,
and his weakness
turned to strength,
his cruelty,
successfully concealed
by his tormenters
lay in wait.

Mousehole

The wind sat in the east
that night,
a howling maw
where the sea should be,
black.
Beyond the harbour lights
a world destroyed,
or might as well be.
Lights that veered
in a water'd eye
on painted streets
and quay
where the stalking horses
of the storm
struggled vainly to be free.
In Wayside's chimney corner
pine logs are piled
against the night.
Behind the heavy curtains
no risks yet to the light.
From warm to gelled air
the spirits come and go
and Wilhelm Reich is walking
round the temples of Khajuraho.

Musee des Beaux Arts

Victorian print
of Penzance Harbour.
"Quite rare,"
the dealer said,
but his price was fair.
To be fair,
the associations
were close in
to time
in Lyonesse.
But the still opportunity
of possession,
and the procession of the light
about the room,
with one moment
just right,
rolled a stone from a gate,
like the unpromising front
to Blackwell's bookshop,
more than all the Turners
in the '75R.A.

Mystery

In the blind alleys
of many cities
the mystery seeps away
in the banal.
No angel, tall elf
or spirit bright
brings a better day.
Why, why
the blessing or
the absence,
who can say?
The hidden gunman
to his visitor
offered a life,
and finding hesitation,
killed both in his sight.

New World

Dido and Aeneas
have quietly slipped
away,
over the wine-dark sea.
Telemachus
has enrolled
for Media Studies.
In the public library
the Loeb Texts,
the same ones I borrowed
forty years ago
are sad and grubby.
Less of them, too.
But now I can borrow
Polish and Albanian
Gujarati and Tamil,
to name but a few.
Do I from sentiment
love a monarch
whose aristocrats
have rotted away?
If the Swedes declare war,
who will crack

their Enigma?
Who will come on
the Brains Trust
and delight us with
their acumen?

Overlooking the Lake

Is night falling?
Can you see to read?
The shadow of Cader
has suddenly taken
the light.
How did what there is
between us
suddenly come
so slight?
All matchings
have their spring
with overwhelming new.
The lane we walked along
has magnolia and yew.
Who can stay
the turning year,
who change now
for then?
And make the strangers
who first met
desire to meet
again?

Palace of the Winds

That straw hat
belongs on the Isis
or the Cam
not Corporation Street
in January.
Still, Psychiatric OP
is used to extravagant attire.
Your old MSc supervisor
whom you sometimes
see in the mirror
may have a little something
for you, providing your elation
remains under control.
That, of course
lost you your last directorship,
last and final,
that is.
Like Pauline, same diagnosis,
whose class mate at Cambridge
still rings her
from the investment bank,
still has her briefly
to stay,
sends her the train fare
to London.

"Read some Dostoyevsky,
it will take you out
of yourself."
But Junior
twenty years younger
had other ideas,
and after two or three sessions
of poker hard pleasuring
put you to work
on the streets of Moss Side.
"You're not cut out for this,"
one kindly punter said
as you spat in the gutter.
Her friend Joe
coughs from the damp
in his basement flat,
quite a reasonable physicist
when he is well,
is starting to have
some movement problems
from the neuroleptics.
Tardive Dyskinesia
I think they call it.

Passive Voice

Chanticleer and
the proud peacock
crow and fan the given,
nor give the anxious cubit
pause for thought.
Form and function germinal
in the egg harry to its keep
the unfettered will
and mock the active voice
with unconscious breath.
And yet
the fecund nothing
from which unthinking
pulse proceeds,
throws beyond the margins
of the drawn
into a place
where a kingdom or a soul
may hang upon
the unknown incline
of a brow.

Patient O

Round and round
and cuss and cuss,
a horizontal Sisyphus.
Straight and straight
and turn and turn.
One bad fling
from Fortune's urn?
Or was some ancient
god provoked
to leave you thus
chained and yoked?
Exemplum
of all our terrors,
in a wilderness
of locker mirrors?
One reminder
from the hatter
that we are but
the slaves of matter.
They say the owl
was a baker's daughter.

Paul

Your head is on one side
as you approach.
Although your course is direct,
your gait is that
of a wanderer.
Charity shops
are favourite destinations,
cheap cafés.
There is never much to spend.
You were doing German at Birkbeck
when the demons came.
They especially love
to kiss the young.
Their timing
is impeccable.
You don't read much Goethe
now.
Your days are like
the distance between planets,
an evening treat
is rented pornography,
shared with friends you met

in Out Patients,
a couple of cans.
You remember from your youth
that freedom
is in the land of dreams.

Pilgrimage

Shipwrecked
and the dent in the sand
soon gone,
you pass the forest
oppressed by mystery.
You pass,
the wind rises,
the trees shake.
Some run and some do not,
the bound kept is
all to the good.
The unlikeliest messengers
bring water and wood,
and point the way.
The length of the night
calls in question the day.

Praeterita

The past is a panther
it hunts us by night
and though it will kill us
it means us no harm.
It stalks us
sidelong
through the woods.
It has the legs
of a god,
it never tires.
Like a deft warrior
it's attack is surprise.
It rises from the sand
and falls like the sea.
Skill may evade,
but only blind chaos
can truly match.
Blind chaos
or a desert.
A monastery,
or an undisturbed garden.

Prisoner's Request

The prisoner
in the observation cell
in the custody block
ceaselessly cried out.
Hour after hour,
rhythmically
like a pulse from a beacon.
"I want to see the staff.
I want to see the staff."
He had been detained
under the Mental Health Act.
Like that prisoner,
I want to see the staff.

Revelation

Beating at doors
long sundered unbeknown,
standing by graves
where the ivy has grown.
Watching through nights
hearing only the wind,
seeking the wise,
finding only the kind.
Sailing through hails
where no light is shown
demanding a voice
hearing only my own.
Watching coals dwindle
till the room has grown cold.
Settling at last
to what I am told.

Saturn Return

Sword in hand
throughout the grove
I hunt
the other me.
It pains me when I think on
the time he's had
to flee.
His sayings, doings, haunt me,
his lack of doing,
more.
It gives me pause to think on
what he might have had
in store.
I thought him gone this thirty years.
Was he merely lying low
in hiding places scarce concealed
where I seldom like to go?
I mean his extirpation,
and the clearing of his ghost;
but my pulse begins to quicken
when his campfire shows him close.

Secrets

Bound about
with adamantine shells,
no infinitesimal
gap
for air or light
to enter.
Fronted
with a chorus smile,
but professionally
applied.
The harlot's clumsiness
would never do.
They sing
in the dry, unlidded
time
when watches change.
For in the breast
of the judge
beats the heart
of a juror,
and on the therapist's
bedroom wall
hangs a portrait of Nietzsche.
Their names
like those

of the ancient
gods
should be written
on tablets
and dropped
in the sea.
And those
that wrote them
put to the sword.

Sic Placet

"Sic Placet," the drunkard said,
and held his placard high.
"It pleases You that
I thus have lived
and in some hovel
die.
I have not shrunk from effort,
I have not shrunk from pain,
endured the lengthy darkness,
borne variety of strain.
But to run and run
forever
however fast or far
and to know that I cannot out run
that one malign star.
Quickness of mind
and eye
nor willingness of heart
were given scope or range
no blessing nor no start.
Let and bar and hindrance
sickness and disdain,
the flourishing of duller men

So You Who set
the stars in place
explain this now to me:
Why should I
and others like me be
unresolved discords
in Your symphony?"

Side Ward

And so it ends.
Eighty years bound in with iron hoops,
keeping in the angst and frisson.
From monochrome beginnings
in a harsh world,
where the city ended
at a farm gate in Longsight,
many burdens,
but strong to bear them.
Striking for a blacksmith,
sometimes striking heads.
Then metal:
metal, measurement, fuel and flight:
War
and the sun going down
behind the Atlas Mountains.
Then a country crossroad
for you more deadly
than Hitler's armies.
Headwound,
and the BSA on its side.
Then forty years of drudgery,
misunderstanding.
And the onlookers

by your bed
like gods
knowing your beginning
and your end.

Species of Oblivion

Tonight, O Lord, the species of oblivion
are present to my mind.
A cold mist fills the house
with the permanence of doom.
The universe itself
has become my room.
The mist which hangs
about this clay,
the sunlight of the morning
will not take away.
Weapons and poison
seem instruments of bliss,
a leap from monstrous height
ends in a lover's kiss.
Like one whom those about him
number several score,
in a crowded hall
sees nothing but the door.
So tonight, Lord,
do not think of me unkind,
though the species of oblivion
are present to my mind.

Spring

The light on the snare drum
tightens, brightens.
Winter dust and ice
flee the tilt of the world.
Springmelt trickles, trembles
tumbles, thunders.
Dust beaten bursts and flies.
The blackbird singing,
piercing pure,
exquisite only
beneath pain,
certain and new as the light
of first creation,
or a sudden angel.
On the Avon,
ducks low hurtle
past jaunty willows.
And sunlit bees work
undisturbed
in a Kentish cottage garden
two valleys from the sea.

The Ancients knew

Dull unburnished gold
that scores a middle way,
Pallas Athene's shield
that pins to still
the great god Dionysus.
Despised of youth and Romance,
the plinth of civic Doric
and colourless First Secretary's
prose,
not to meet you
along the way
is to die in an alley.
Beneath the cowl
you ground
ecstasy
and drop by drop
enliven
the soil beneath
endeavour.

The Lane at Glenmore

This peerless
Cooley mountain morning,
let us lament
a butterfingered God
who dropped
Paradise
allowing it to shatter infinitesimally,
leaving beauty`s
jagged edge.
In the time
of the famine,
families climbing the lane
past the sisters O`Neill,
faces of snot
from the grass,
without the strength
for the mountain
and Carlingford
and the hope of the sea.

The Power of Meaning

Led by toys,
given no arrows,
carrying only a spear,
the quest to mean
may not sail plane.
Not all may tell
the courses of the stars
or cast baptistery doors.
Coloured robes
and unmarked graves,
cells and watchtowers,
may enclose
the leaden flower
that cannot help
but grow.
Within the circle
of the moon
now the Romans,
now barbarians
may have the higher ground,
and the same hill top
with a beacon
for a moment
spark.
But in a place

beyond places,
whence comes the beauty
of the stars,
reposes harbour,
and a road
inland,
which we will understand
when we know whence
comes the impulse to
wilderness,
and delight in whales
in distant seas.

Tree

In the beginning
the serpent's gift
was not the apple
but the head,
the face first seen
in Eden's stream,
suddenly snatched away
then slow return,
to gaze and know,
the barter for
endless sky and sea,
untold world and worlds.
And the first digging stick
through the first heart,
and the first monkey's head
on a man,
to see if they can,
to see if they can.
And if all goes well,
then they can tell,
and with infinite patience pick
at the locks that hold in Hell.

Tremadog Bay August 30th

The temptation of Faust
is calling,
to ask for the words
to tell,
the blue-white of the sea
this morning.
Should I dance
on the lid of Hell?
I fumble at Capri
and Paphos,
struck dumb by cerulean
skies.
From such a sea as this
did Aphrodite rise.
Though I plead
with the Muses
for succour,
and lay on their altar
my plight,
their silence tells me this morning
I have had my mede of light.

But the Devil
ever watchful
has come on to the beach,
and on yellow sands
holds golden keys
ten feet out of reach.

Untitled

Hairs un-numbered,
sparrows uncounted,
mathematics may not tell
of Your remove.
The unburied dead
meld slowly
into the ground,
like fallen sheep
on a distant moor,
the flesh running
like slow water.
Then bones,
then nothing.
Unfathomable
the caprice
of Your emissaries,
now absent,
now plucking out.

Untitled (2)

Brick by golden brick
my gaol grew tall and strong,
cemented by my choosings
and the pledgings
of my tongue.
My pleasures were
my felonies,
my duties,
torts and wrongs;
few prisons lack
for shafts of light
and early morning songs.
My friendships were
the halls and stairs
where prisoners
might pass,
and greet from time to time
hands against the glass.
Custom set
the course of things,
and blocked off
airy ways.
Obligation turned the key
and ordered all my days.
But still in thought

the mountains rise
that childish maps
did show,
and distant waters sparkle,
and distant waters flow.

Untitled (3)

Eaglets and egyptologists
have the right idea:
put two together
see one below.
He who would brook
and bourne,
leave his blood on the snow.
The Lord God cast
the spark
onto each soul's floor.
Breach not my walls, break not my door.
Lucy Morgan
simple, put on,
no-one took her part.
When she had to
took a dagger,
drew it through a heart.

Valencia

Ten days on from
winter in Valencia,
what remains?
Beyond the forest
of cranes gradually
hauling the eld
of northern Europe
into Mediterranean light?
The lofty rocky fastness
of Guadalest,
long deserted by the Moors
desertedly airy in the cold,
above the olives
and the almonds.
But most of all
the sanctuary of
Fuentesanta
over Murcia
where peace and glory
seemed woven
into the quiet sunlight;
the cavernous basilica
of Elche charged

with stillness.
Or so it seemed
to the cold northern eye
of a cold northern shore.

Visiting Time

"I had a good man,"
the old lady said,
with the Sister,
in the side ward,
in the silence.
In the corridors
a full-fed generation
raucous
heads for the bus stop,
the car park.
The buses pass
on Oxford Road
and the Hacienda gets going
for the night.

"Vous etes Belge, Monsieur?"

He sought the language of God,
to speak and be
one of His own.
He roamed the lands thought
to be His,
and questioned His people,
as they were known.
"Vous etes Belge, Monsieur,
Vous etes Belge?"
He journeyed from Lille to Sorbonne,
sat at the feet of professors,
he clawed at the hill of truth,
besieged its soi-disant possessors.
"Vous etes Belge, Monsieur,
Vous etes Belge?"
He embraced the Academy's
defining,
spoke in prayer and meditation:
turned aside from intellect,
clung to the tail of revelation,
found himself grown old
in the practice of articulation.
"Vous etes Belge, Monsieur,
Vous etes Belge?"

Wheel

Take me down
to the sea of souls
where lots are cast
for the ways of men.
Show the retorts
through which they pass
to make them wish
to rise again.
Reveal if you can
sub specie what,
do they yea-say to the close?
Zarathustra bathing in the winter stream,
which Nietzsche wrote as he froze.
The beggars by the Ganges
walking on all fours,
the lepers at Swayambhunath,
the dollar-fifty whores.

Zu ende

So we lifted a glass
and considered
how their kind had passed away,
the authenticist
the grammarian
indifferent to pay.
Stick on a point of Old English
elocution,
live and die in the
Athenian constitution.
Make the ordered life
the work,
sing evensong in
an empty church.

Mot Juste

Mock mountains mock,
and with your folded light
deride,
all those who sing
of wind and tide.
Watch the poor
rhymer
run to get
his rapture
in a butterfly net.
Will the future
solely
"spring form the furrows."
of the calculating Burroughs?
A full stop
to all the fuss,
nihil
ex omnibus,
encompassing the dead
and the quick,
between the Zen master's
pupil
and the Zen master's stick.

Elgar Girl

Birch beautiful,
the shires in your bones,
you said your heart
was frozen when we met
from captivity
in a cold place.
But the night
in Hay
that they should play
the Elgar Cello,
of all things.
"This was meant to be,"
you said,
"This was meant to be."
From midnight
to the second hour,
fire,
fire.